the essential string method

violin *book one*

Sheila M. Nelson

with

Catherine Elliott
Gerald Howard
Adrian Thorn

Design
Susan Clarke

Illustrations
Phylip Harries
Valerie Hill
Martine Blaney

Hoe Down (pages 7, 12, 19 & 23) is from *New Tunes for Strings* by Stanley Fletcher and Paul Rolland,

BOOSEY & HAWKES

Boosey & Hawkes Music Publishers Ltd
www.boosey.com

Contents

These signs will remind you to:

sing

get ready, then play

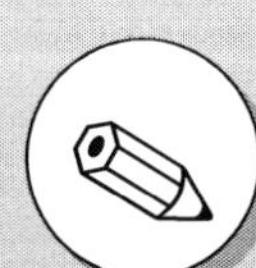

write

avoid a frying-pan hand

check your bow hold

STAGE 1 Strings and their names

Naming the strings

Look at the **blue pages** in the middle of the book to see how to hold your violin and name its strings.

Make up sentences to include an **E**lephant, an **A**lligator, a **D**onkey or a **G**oat.

Find the string that goes with each animal, then sing and play your sentences on your violin.

Say 'shh' or pretend to blow out a candle between the notes you play.

New Waltz *

When you play this tune (plucking or bowing), copy the way your teacher makes a wide circle with his or her right hand whenever you see this sign:

* *A highlighted title indicates that a piece has an accompaniment, available in a separate book.*

Tapping the pulse

Like people, music has a pulse. It goes on and on without stopping.

Sometimes a musical pulse beats quickly, just as your heart does when you have been running. Sometimes it beats more slowly, as your heart does if you are sitting quietly.

Choose a song you know well and decide whether you are going to sing it quickly or slowly. Tap a regular beat and then start to sing. Keep tapping the beat all through the song.

Chocolate Treats (**d**oh **s**oh)

Learn to sing this with your teacher.

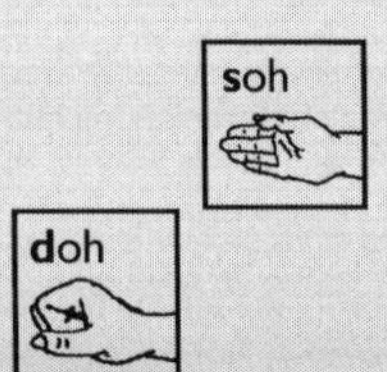

d **s** **d**
Choc'- late treats,

d **s** **d**
Choc'- late treats.

d d d d **s s s s**
Um-pa-lum-pa, um-pa-lum-pa,

d **s** **d**
Choc'- late treats.

Pebbling a song

The rhythm of a piece of music is made up of shorter and longer notes, faster and slower notes. You can see this if you try 'pebbling'.

First, find lots of pebbles. Counters, buttons or beads will do just as well. Sing *Chocolate Treats* and put down a pebble for each word or part of a word that you sing, making a line of pebbles.

Now sing the song again. Point to the pebbles as you sing. You will find that sometimes you go quite slowly from one pebble to the next, and sometimes you go more quickly.

This pattern is called the rhythm and is often different from the pulse.

You can do this with any of your favourite songs.

Can you find the two sounds *Chocolate Treats* uses on your violin?

Try playing the tune as you sing it.

Happy and sad violinists!

There are pictures of violinists all the way through this book.

Some are happy because they are holding their violins and bows well.

Others are sad because they are not holding their violins and bows well.

See if you can say which violinists are happy, which are sad and why. Answers on page 28.

Marching

Learn to sing *Marching* with your teacher.
Play the bars with notes. Sing the bars in between (see page 27).

Raining (doh soh)

Learn to sing *Raining* with your teacher.
Can you find the two sounds it uses on your violin?

d d s s d d s
Rain - ing here and rain - ing there,

d d d d s s s
Rain - ing al - most ev - ' ry-where.

d d d s s d d d s
Rain-ing for ducks and rain-ing for frogs,

s s s s d d d
Oh is's rain - ing cats and dogs.

Checklist

✔ When you can
- ❑ play New Waltz
- ❑ tap the pulse as you sing a song
- ❑ sing Chocolate Treats and play it on your violin
- ❑ sing and play Marching
- ❑ sing Raining and play it on your violin

✔ When you have
- ❑ made up and played lots of sentences on your violin
- ❑ pebbled Chocolate Treats

STAGE 2 Using the bow

Bowing

The **blue pages** remind you how to hold the bow, and how to get ready to play.

James the mouse

James the mouse will help you to learn a good bow hold. As you can see from the pictures below, James has a special place where he likes to sit.

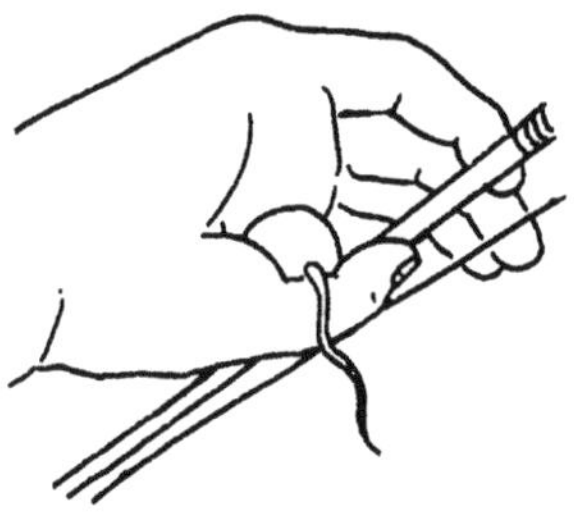

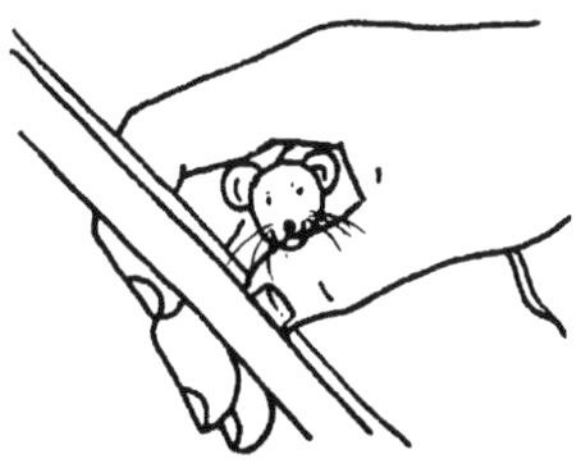

Try not to squash James when you play the violin. Whenever you see a picture of him, check your bow hold!

Try playing the rhythm of these sentences on your violin, using the bow:

My name is ____________________

I like eating ____________________

My favourite game is ______________

Now go back to the sentences you made up on page 3. Try playing them with your bow, matching the strings to the animals.

As you get used to holding the bow and the violin you can try bowing the pieces you learnt in Stage 1: *New Waltz*, *Chocolate Treats*, *Marching* and *Raining*.

Bow games

Can you do these things and still hold your bow well?

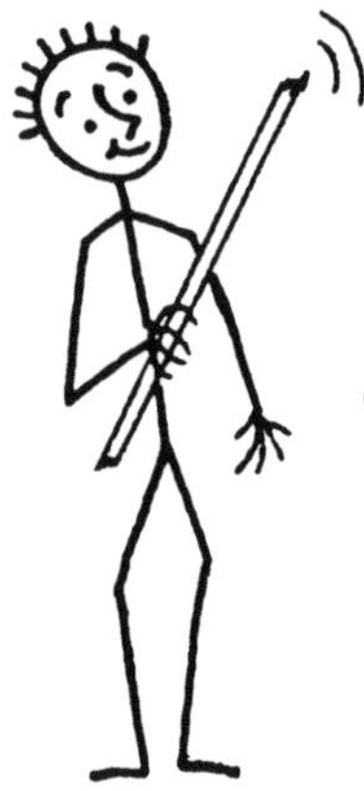

Turn your bow into a windscreen wiper.

Plant a bow tree in the ground.

Stir a magic pot.

Tap-and-say

Make a set of rhythm cards. Do this with an adult as you will need scissors, an old breakfast cereal box and a felt pen.

Cut up the cereal box to make 20 cards, each about 6 cm x 10 cm.

Draw ♩ on 8 cards.

Draw ♫ on 8 cards.

Draw 𝄽 on 4 cards.

Ta **ti-ti** **Ma**

To make your own rhythm you will need to:

1. Shuffle your cards and lay some out in a line to make a rhythm.
2. Decide on the pulse of the music and tap it steadily. Then, continuing to tap the pulse, say the names of the cards. You should find yourself moving to a new card with each tap. (If you find this hard at first, someone else can tap the pulse while you say the names and point to the cards.)
3. Shuffle the cards again and make a new rhythm to tap-and-say.

Count the rests (𝄽) in the last line or find an action for them: walk, sway or bend your knees in time to the beat.

Hoe Down

Learn the chorus from memory. You will add more verses later on. Count the beats of the introduction before you begin: 1 2, 1 2.

Snowman (soh mi)

Learn to sing the *Snowman* song with your teacher.

s		**m**		**s**	**s**	**m**
Snow	-	man		melt	a -	way.
s	**s**	**m**	**m**	**s**	**s**	**m**
Snow-flakes		fall - ing		fast	and	free?
s	**s**	**m**	**m**	**s**	**s**	**m**
Now	the	sun	comes	out	to	play,
s		**m**		**s**	**s**	**m**
Snow	-	man		melt	a -	way.

Sometimes sing *Snowman* to the words and sometimes to the solfa names.
Can you make the handsigns too?

Finding a rhythm

1. When you know *Snowman* by heart, clap the rhythm and 'pebble' it.
2. The rhythm of *Snowman* uses two patterns you already know: long ♩ and little ♫ notes. See if you can lay out your rhythm cards to show the pattern of long and little notes in *Snowman*.
   The beginning should look like this:

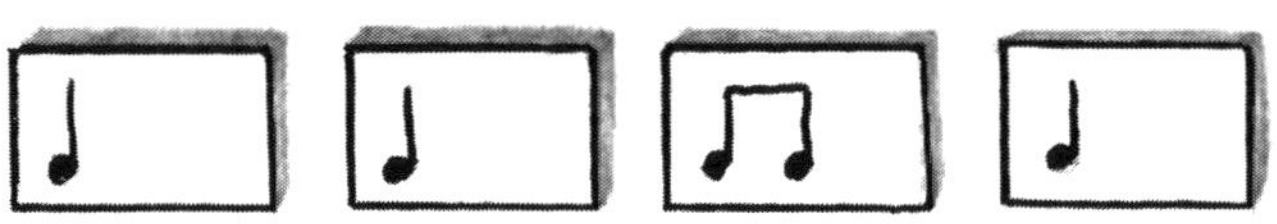

3. **Tap** the pulse and **say** the rhythm on your cards to check that it really sounds like the song.

4. Play the rhythm of *Snowman* on your violin. Choose any open string you like.

Take care to use little bows for ti-ti and longer bows for Ta.

Happy or sad?

More tunes to play

Find Open String Tunes in the **activities pages**. See if you can play *Pease Pudding*, *Spacemen* and *Cowboy Chorus*.

New Waltz Variations

These are variations on *New Waltz*, which you learnt in Stage 1. Learn some or all of them now. Don't forget to keep on playing them right through the book.

Can you think of any more variations to play?

Happy or sad?

Checklist

✔ When you can

- ❑ play Stage 1 pieces with the bow
- ❑ tap the pulse and say rhythms from your rhythm cards
- ❑ play Hoe Down, verse 1, with the chorus from memory
- ❑ sing Snowman by heart
- ❑ play Pease Pudding as a duet
- ❑ play Spacemen as a duet
- ❑ play Cowboy Chorus as a duet
- ❑ play New Waltz Variation 1

✔ When you have

- ❑ played sentences with your bow
- ❑ played bow games
- ❑ made a set of rhythm cards
- ❑ worked out the rhythm of Snowman
- ❑ played Musical copycats

Musical copycats

Listen to the pattern your teacher or a friend plays on the violin.

Try copying it.

Sometimes you should make up a pattern for them to copy. You can use any string.

STAGE 3 Sing, swing and play

Swing as You Play

When you play this tune make sure your bowing elbow swings **up** to play the **lower** notes, and **down** for the **higher** notes.

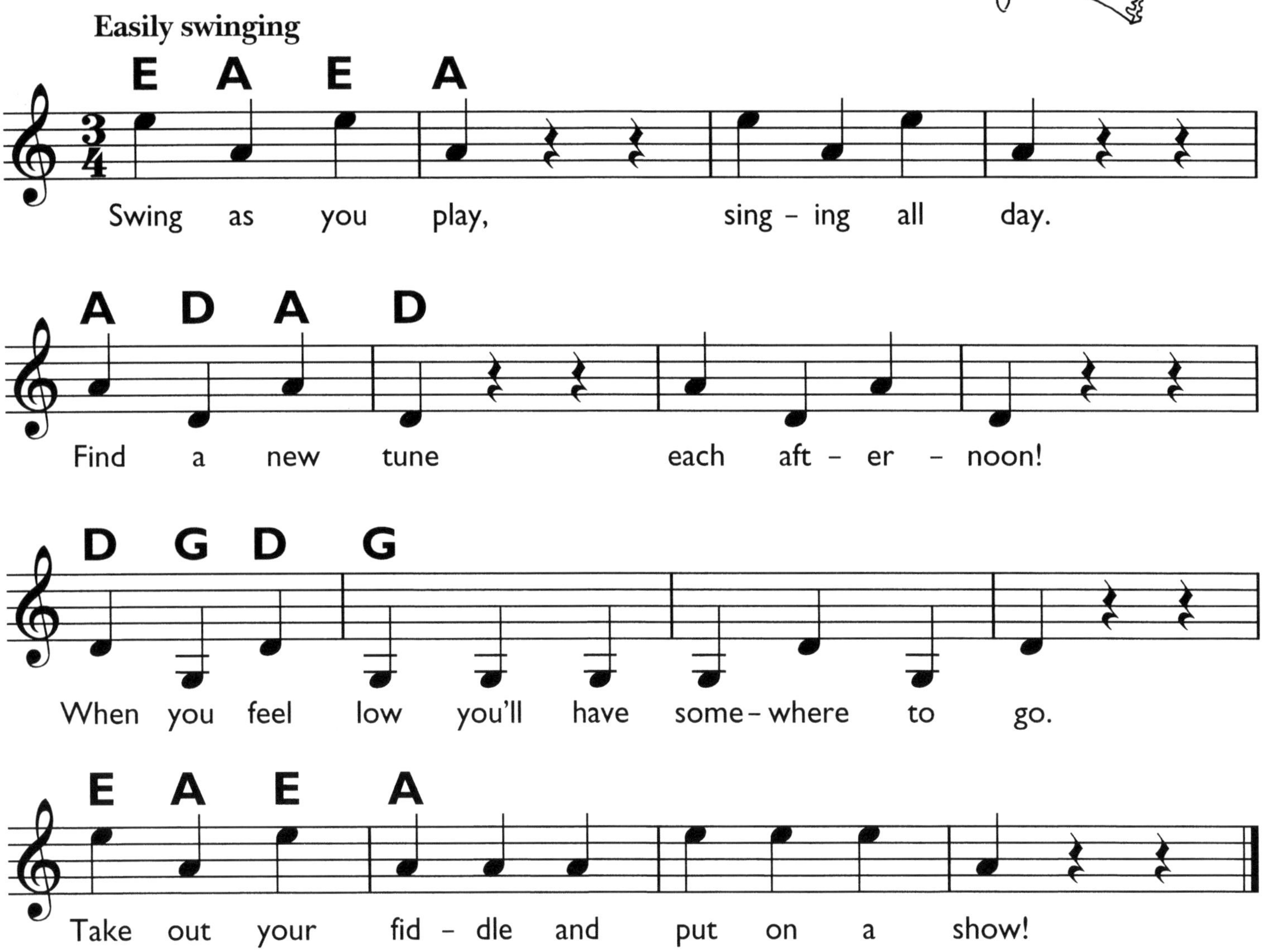

Left-hand fingers

Soon it will be time to use your left-hand fingers to make different notes on the violin. To discover the correct position for this hand, turn to the **blue pages** and learn how to position your left-hand fingers on a pencil. Practise doing this, ready for Stage 4.

More tunes to play

Find Open String Tunes on the **activities pages** and play:

Circles

Twinkle Twinkle.

And don't forget the *New Waltz Variations* on page 9.

Singing and writing Snowman

Sing the *Snowman* song by heart (page 8), using the solfa names. It is made up of two sounds: a higher one (**s**oh) and a lower one (**m**i).

Sing it again and each time you sing **s**oh draw a note **above** the line. Each time you sing **m**i draw a note **below** the line. The first four notes have been filled in for you.

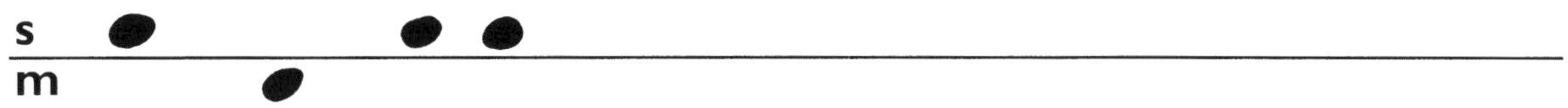

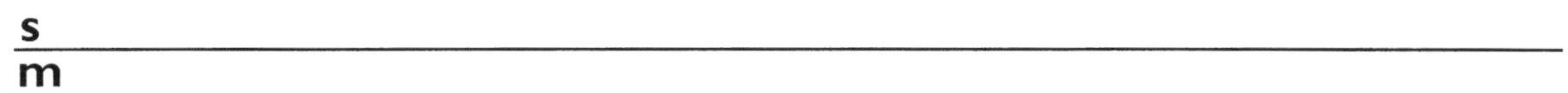

A Mugs Game (soh mi)

See if you can sing this new song.
First say the rhythm names and then the words in rhythm.
Now try singing the song.

Remind yourself how **s**oh and **m**i sound by singing the beginning of *Snowman*.

See our mugs on the wall. Some are tall, some are small. Here's my fav -'rite one of all.

Half Past Three

Write the names of the strings above the notes.

Sing the tune (words, note names or solfa).

Now play the tune on your violin.

Happy or sad?

Hungrily

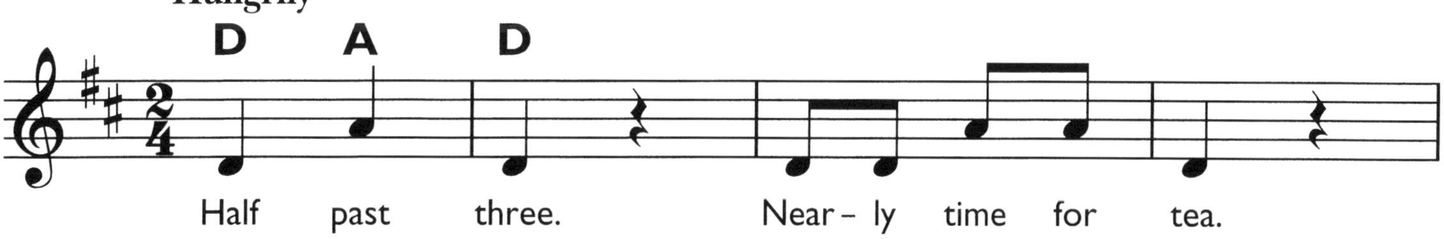

Low D, High D

Learn to sing *Low D, High D* with your teacher.
Touch the ground when you sing low D and stretch up when you sing high D.

Low D, high D, ground D, sky D.

Aer - o - planes can fly, stay up in the sky.

Down they come to land in a - ny dis-tant town, but the

Sun and the moon and stars are al - ways up on high.

Hoe Down, verse 2

Here is verse 2 of *Hoe Down* (page 7). Play the chorus after each verse.

Now play the CHORUS from memory

Checklist

✔ When you can
- ❑ play Swing as You Play
- ❑ read and sing A Mugs Game from the music
- ❑ read and play Half Past Three
- ❑ sing Low D, High D by heart
- ❑ play Hoe Down, verse 2

✔ When you have
- ❑ shaped your left-hand fingers on a pencil
- ❑ played Circles as a duet
- ❑ played Twinkle Twinkle as a duet
- ❑ played New Waltz Variations
- ❑ made Snowman on the one-line stave

STAGE 4 Left-hand fingers

Two-a-Penny

Play the lines marked with two plums for now.

Your teacher will play the lines marked with a penny.

Happy or sad?

Lunchtime sentences

Make up and sing some sentences about what you like to eat for lunch, using the sounds low D and high D.

Look at the **blue pages** to see how to place your left-hand fingers on the violin. Try playing lunchtime sentences. For example:

A string			3	3	3
D string	0	0			
	I	*like*	*sau - sa*	*-*	*ges*

Making notes and a two-line stave

Do this with an adult as you will need scissors, a large cereal box, a felt pen and a ruler.

Cut the cereal box to make a long, wide strip of cardboard. Cut the rest into as many note heads as you can, 35mm wide and 25mm tall.

Using the felt pen and the ruler, draw two parallel lines down the centre of the blank side of the strip of cardboard, 25mm apart.

Musical questions and answers

Listen to the question your teacher or friend plays on the violin. Now make up an answer.

Sometimes you should make questions for them to answer.

Low D, High D

As fast as you can sing the words!

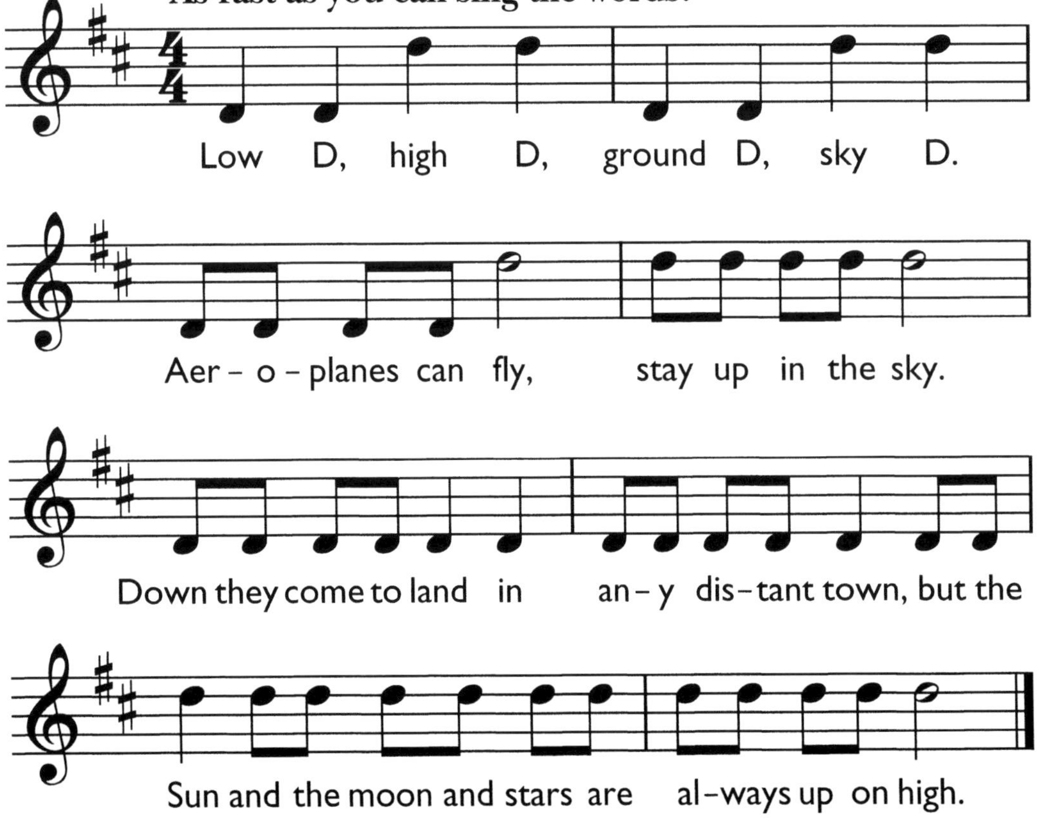

New notes on the A string

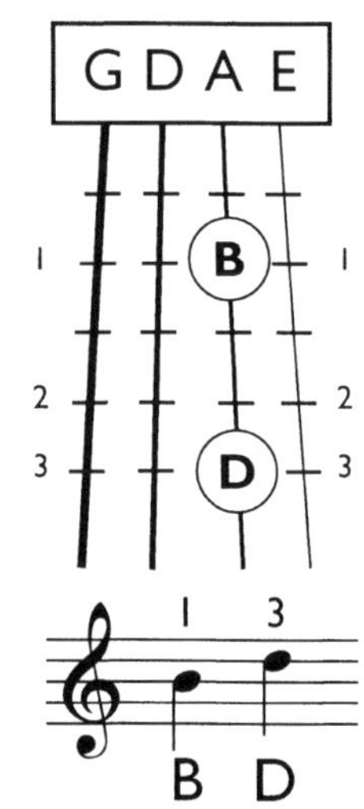

Now turn to page 15.

Activities Pages

Marching Scale

Waltzing Scale

Open String Tunes

These tunes can be played as a duet with your teacher or with a friend. The page number of the second part is given in brackets.

Cowboy Chorus (page 21 – **d**oh is D)

D D D D	G G G G	D D D D	A A A A
D D D D	G G G G	D D A A	D D

Spacemen (page 16)

A A A	E E E
A A A A A	E 𝄽 𝄽
A A A A A	E E E E E
A A D A	A 𝄽 𝄽

Circles (page 22)

D A D A	D A D A
D D G D	A A A 𝄽
D A D A	D A D A
D D A A	D D D 𝄽

A E A E	A E A E
A A D A	E E E E
A E A E	A E A E
A A E E	E A A 𝄽

Pease Pudding (opposite)

D D D D 𝄽
G G G D 𝄽
D D D D D D
A A D 𝄽

Twinkle, Twinkle (opposite)

D D D D	G G D –	G G D D	A A D –
D D A A	D D A –	D D A A	D D A –
D D D D	G G D –	G G D D	A A D –

Happy or sad?

Criss-Cross (overleaf)

Pluck with your left little finger. **Bold** notes in the low position near to the pegs, normal notes as high up the fingerboard as possible.

G G G G	𝄽 𝄽 𝄽 𝄽	**E E** E E	𝄽 𝄽 𝄽 𝄽
G G E E	𝄽 𝄽 𝄽 𝄽	**E E** G G	𝄽 𝄽 𝄽 𝄽
G G E G	𝄽 𝄽 𝄽 𝄽	**E G** G E	𝄽 𝄽 𝄽 𝄽
G E **G** E	𝄽 𝄽 𝄽 𝄽	**E** G **E** E	**G** G **G** 𝄽

Holding the bow

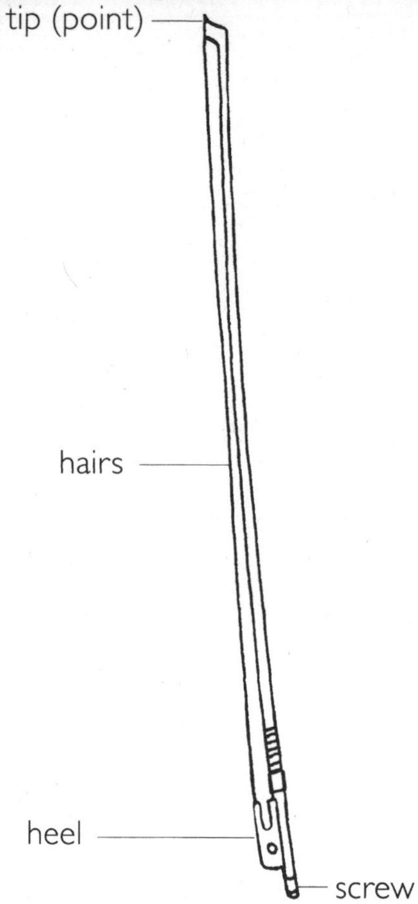

Care of your bow
Before playing, slightly tighten the hairs on the bow by turning the screw at the heel. Remember to loosen them before putting your violin away.

1 Hold your right arm in front of you and let the **right hand** dangle down naturally (not stiffly) from the wrist. This is how it will look when holding the bow.

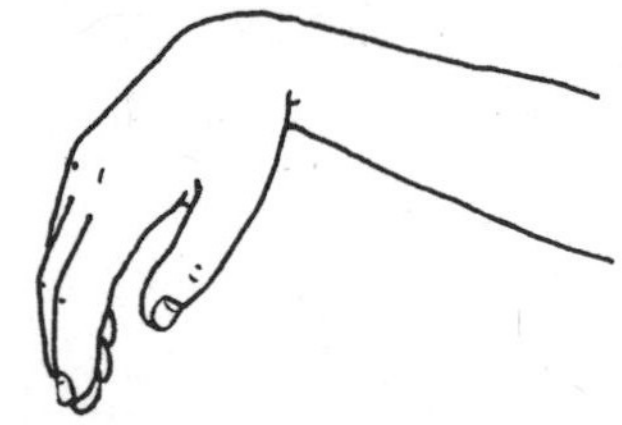

2 Now turn it over.

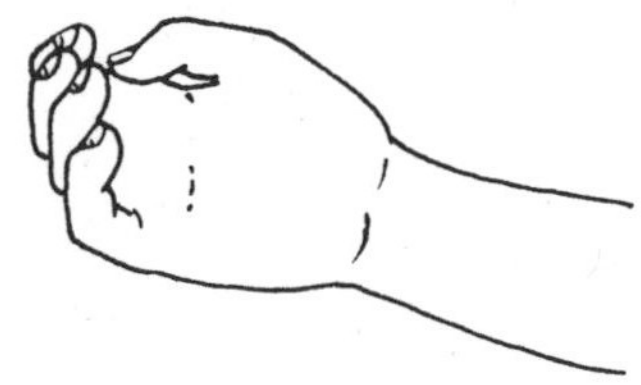

3 Take a pencil with your **left hand** and place it across the right hand from the tip of the little finger to the end line on the first finger, without changing their position.

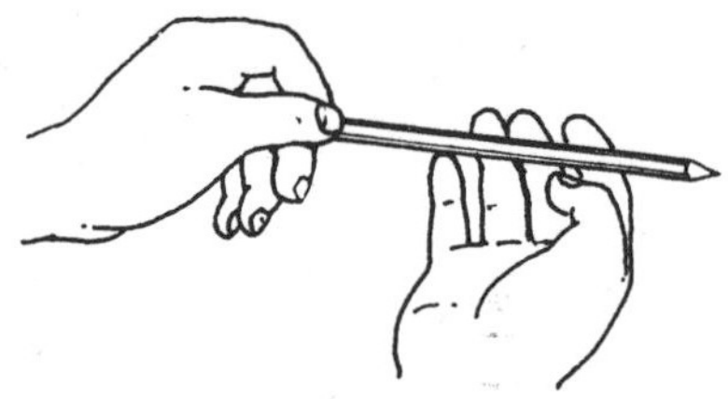

4 Touch the pencil very lightly with the corner of your thumb nail at about the middle of the fingers. Turn your hand over, hang the wrist again and you have your first bow hold.

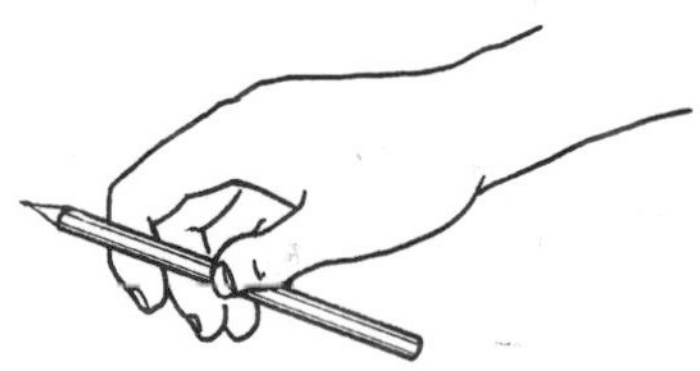

5 Space the fingers a little apart with a left-hand fingertip.

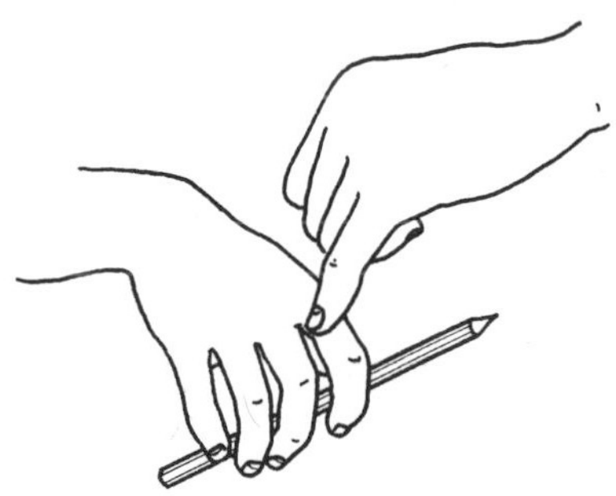

6 When all this feels easy, go back to step 1, using the bow instead of the pencil. Hold the bow a little way from the heel so that it feels very light.

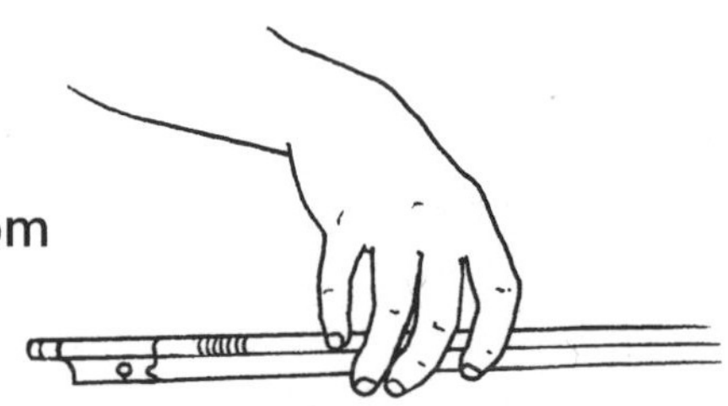

You can hold the bow like this for the first few weeks. Later, you will learn to hold the bow at the heel, with the tip of your little finger resting on the side of the bow nearest to you.

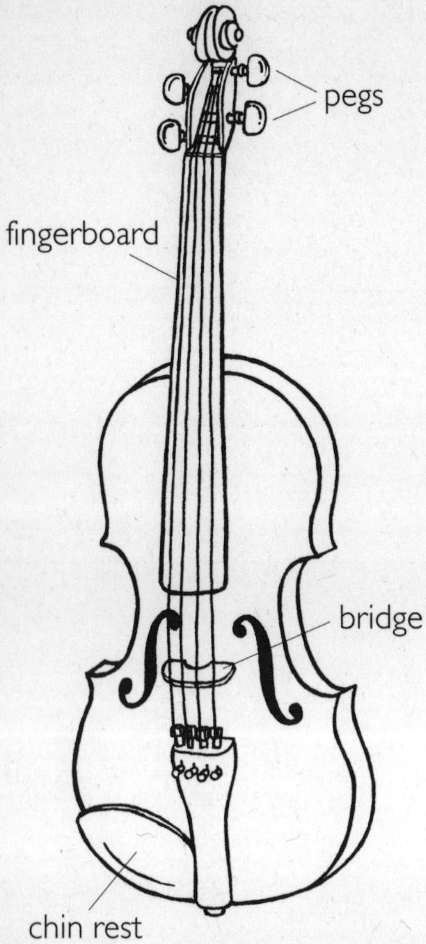

1 Can you feel your collarbone with the tips of your fingers? It is like a little shelf on which you can rest your violin.

2 Stand with your feet slightly apart. Holding your violin with both hands, like the person in the picture, lift it up high. Make sure both of your hands are the same height so that the violin is level.

3 Now gently lower your violin on to its little shelf. Make sure it is tucked in very close to your neck.

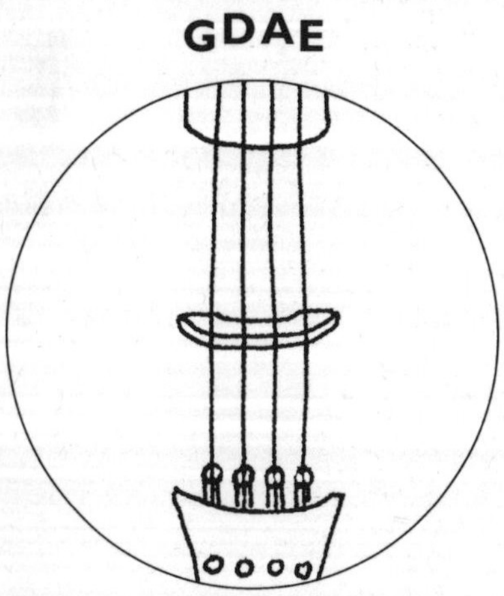

4 Turn your head a little bit towards the chin rest. Check that the pegs and the chin rest are on the same level. This is a good way to hold the violin for open string pieces.

5 Can you wiggle your left elbow so that your little finger can pluck the string furthest away from it? Try to do this every time you pick up your violin. It will help your shoulder to feel loose and relaxed – not all hunched up.

1 Hold the violin under your right arm, as shown in the picture.

2 Remembering how you practised on a pencil, let the three longest fingers of your left hand rest on the fingerboard with the thumb touching gently at its natural position.

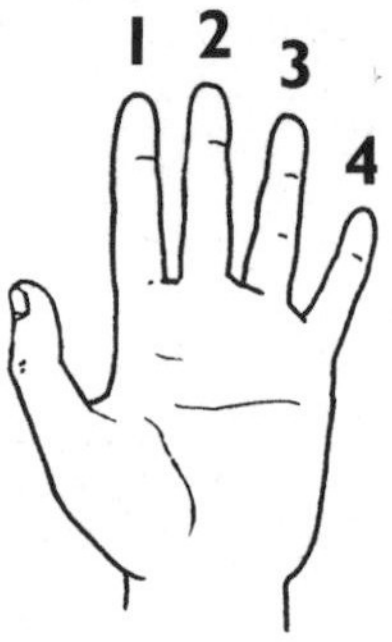

3 Press the A string down to the fingerboard with fingers 1 2 and 3. Pluck the D string twice with your right thumb, then the A string twice. Does it sound like the start of *Low D, High D*?

If the sound is not right, you need to **'tune your left hand'** by moving it up towards the bridge or down towards the pegs a little. Don't change the hand shape at all, but slide the whole hand by moving your arm. Your teacher will help you, and just at first you may need a little marker stuck on to the fingerboard.

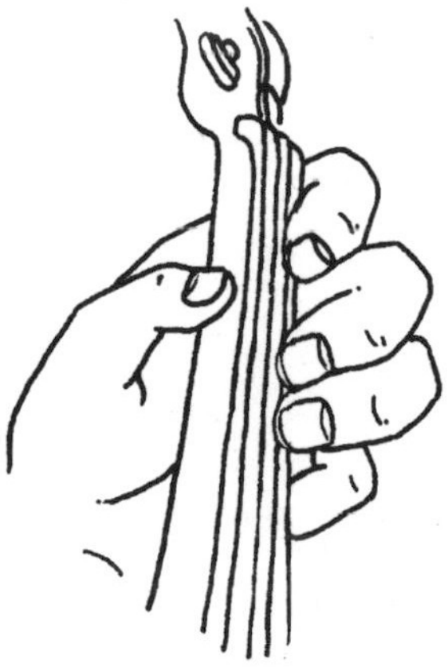

4 When the sound is correct for the beginning of *Low D, High D*, push back your first finger a little.

5 Move the violin up onto its shelf without changing your fingers, and you are ready to play.

1 Take up the violin, using both hands to place it on its shelf.

2 Gently take up the bow and rest the hairs of the bow on the strings of the violin while you find your bow hold. Feel the inside of your middle two fingers touching the bow, and be careful not to hook your first finger right over. It is not supposed to hold up the bow.

3 If you need your left-hand fingers, tune your hand.

Positioning your left hand

1 Hold a pencil at one end with your **right hand**.

Hold up your **left hand** with the palm facing you, the fingers falling over in a relaxed, natural way and the thumb pointing upwards at the side.

2 Slide the pencil under the tips of the three longest fingers without separating them, letting the thumb touch gently at its natural position.

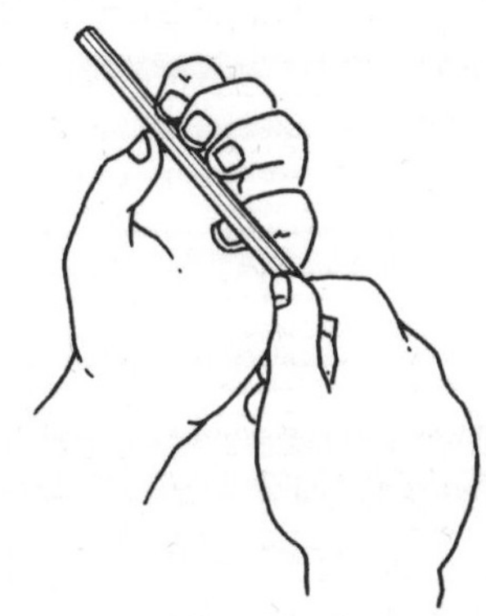

3 Turn your hand a little until the side of your first finger touches the pencil. Now try to slide the tip of the first finger back from the others without changing anything else.

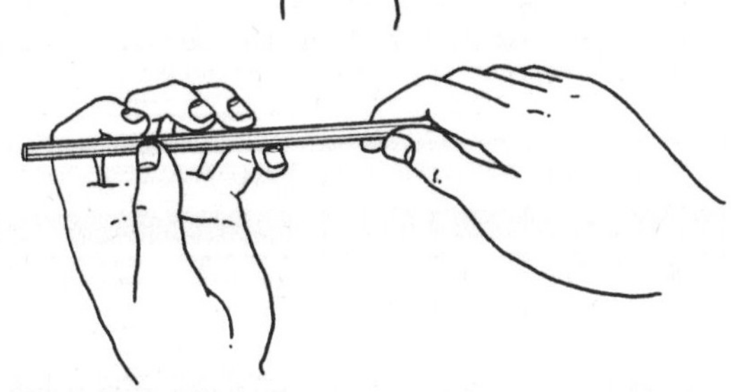

If this seems difficult at first, you will need to practise polishing that little strip of pencil with your fingertip. The space between the first and second fingers will be important in all of the music you play in this book.

Get Your Fingers Working

These tunes can be played on any string.

Merrily We Roll Along

2 1 0 1	2 2 2 –	1 1 1 –	2 2 2 –
2 1 0 1	2 2 2 –	1 1 2 1	0 – 𝄽 𝄽

The Grand Old Duke of York

2 1 0 0 0 0	0 – 𝄽 0
1 1 1 1	1 – 𝄽 1
2 2 2 2 2	3 3 3 3 3 3
2 2 1 1	0 – 𝄽

Pease Pudding (opposite)

0 0 1 2 𝄽
3 3 3 2 𝄽
0 0 1 2 2 2
1 1 0 𝄽

These tunes use two strings next to each other:
a lower one and a higher one.

Twinkle, Twinkle (opposite)

0 0 0 0	1 1 0 –	3 3 2 2	1 1 0 –
0 0 3 3	2 2 1 –	0 0 3 3	2 2 1 –
0 0 0 0	1 1 0 –	3 3 2 2	1 1 0 –

Lavender's Blue

0 0 0	0 3 2 1 0	0 1 1	1 𝄽 𝄽
0 0 0	0 3 2 1 0	3 2 1	0 𝄽 𝄽

(When playing *Pease Pudding* and *Twinkle, Twinkle* as a duet, start on the open D string.)

All Aboard

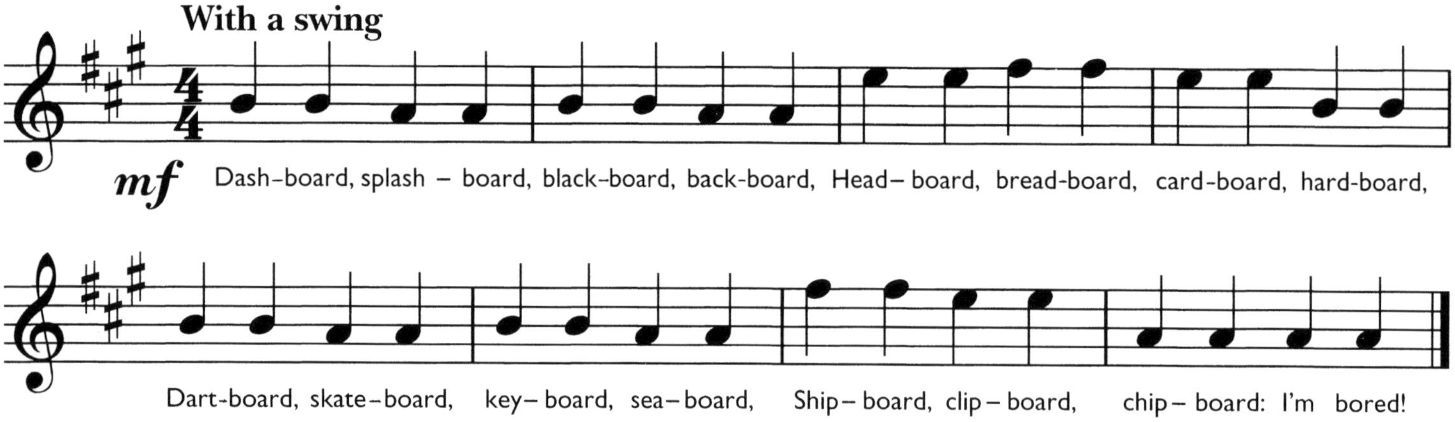

VARIATIONS

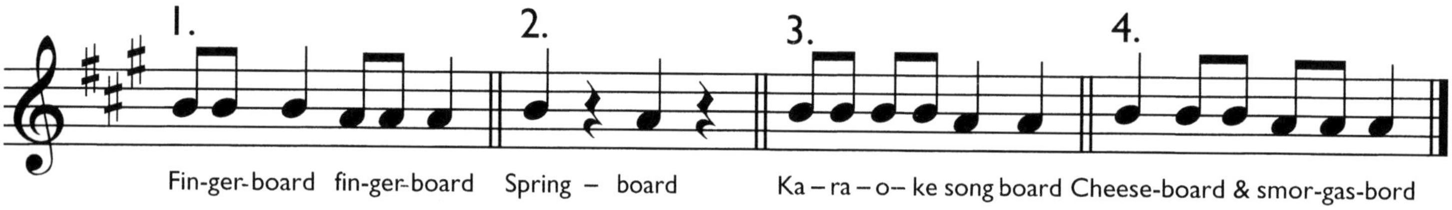

Criss-Cross (for swinging elbows)

Pluck all the notes marked + with your left-hand little finger. The normal notes should be played with your hand near the pegs. For the 'x' notes your hand should be as high up the fingerboard as possible. The bowed notes are added later on.

Singing and writing A Mugs Game

Happy or sad?

The notes **s**oh and **m**i are copycats. If one sits on a line, so will the other. If one sits in a space, so will the other. Notice that **s**oh is higher than **m**i.

When you wrote out *Snowman*, you drew the notes in the spaces above and below the line, but **s**oh and **mi** can also be on two lines.

Sing *A Mugs Game* and see if you can finish drawing notes to make the tune on the two lines below. The first six notes have been drawn for you.

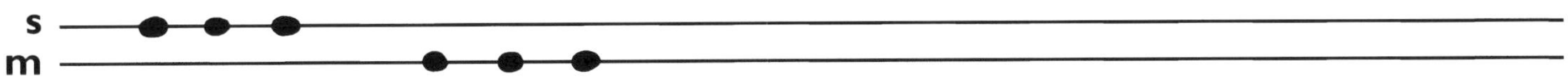

On your own stave you can make a **s**oh **m**i tune of your own. You can place the two notes in the spaces either side of a line, or on two lines next to one another. It doesn't matter, as long as **s**oh is higher than **m**i. Sing your tune to everyone at home.

Playing Snowman

Have a go at playing *Snowman*. Use the third finger of your left hand for the **s**oh sounds and your first finger for the **m**i sounds.

Play the beginning of *Low D, High D* to 'tune your hand'.

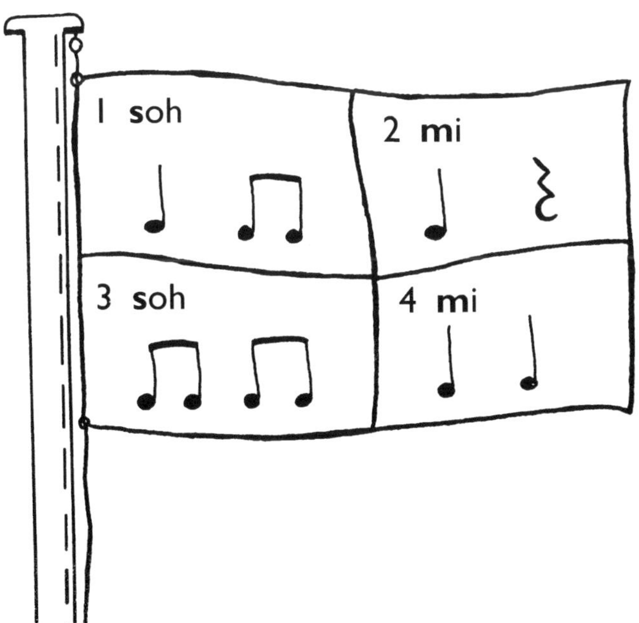

Flag Tunes

1. To perform a Flag Tune sing or play round the numbered squares in order, using the rhythm and sound in each square.
2. Draw a flag and make your own Flag Tune by writing a sound and a rhythm in each square.
3. Now perform your Flag Tune for your Mum, Dad or a friend. Show your flag to your teacher.

Mobile rhythms

Have a rhythm conversation with a friend.

1. Tap a regular beat with your friend, making sure you are exactly together. Your friend should keep on tapping while you get ready to say your rhythm message.
2. Say your rhythm, in time to the pulse, and when you have finished start tapping with your friend and say 'Your turn'.
3. Your friend now answers with a new rhythm and hands over to you with 'Your turn'.

Use a mixture of these patterns: 

Spacemen (doh ray)

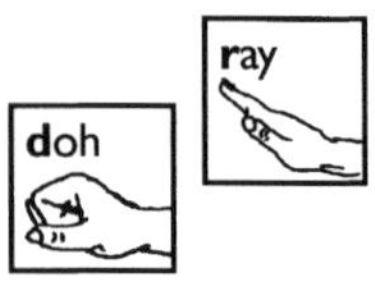

Sing *Spacemen* to the words, and to solfa.

Now try playing it.

Fairly fast

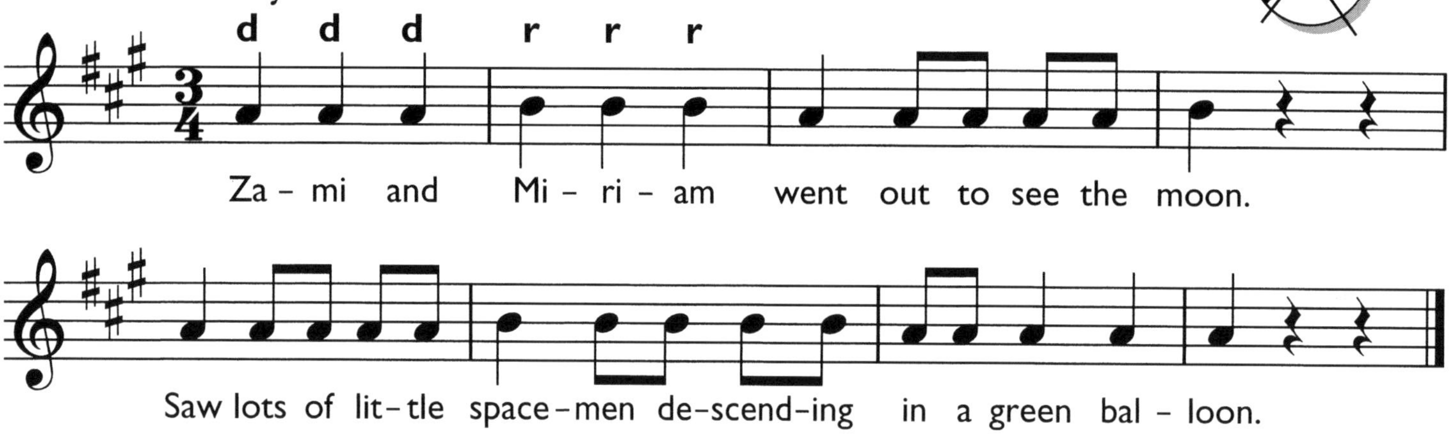

Happy or sad?

Happy or sad?

Checklist

✔ When you can
- ❑ play Two-a-Penny
- ❑ play Low D, High D
- ❑ play Snowman
- ❑ sing and play Spacemen

✔ When you have
- ❑ sung and played Lunchtime sentences
- ❑ made notes and a two-line stave
- ❑ played Musical questions and answers
- ❑ written down and played A Mugs Game
- ❑ made up and played a Flag Tune
- ❑ played Mobile rhythms

Getting your fingers working

Animal sentences

It is time to get your fingers working! Make up an animal sentence.

Think of a:	*(example)*
colour	*purple*
animal	*elephant*
action	*playing*
place	*park*

Example: *Purple elephants playing in the park.*

Have four goes at playing your animal sentence on any string you like. Start with your third finger and lift off a finger between each go. Then play a new sentence.

Carousel

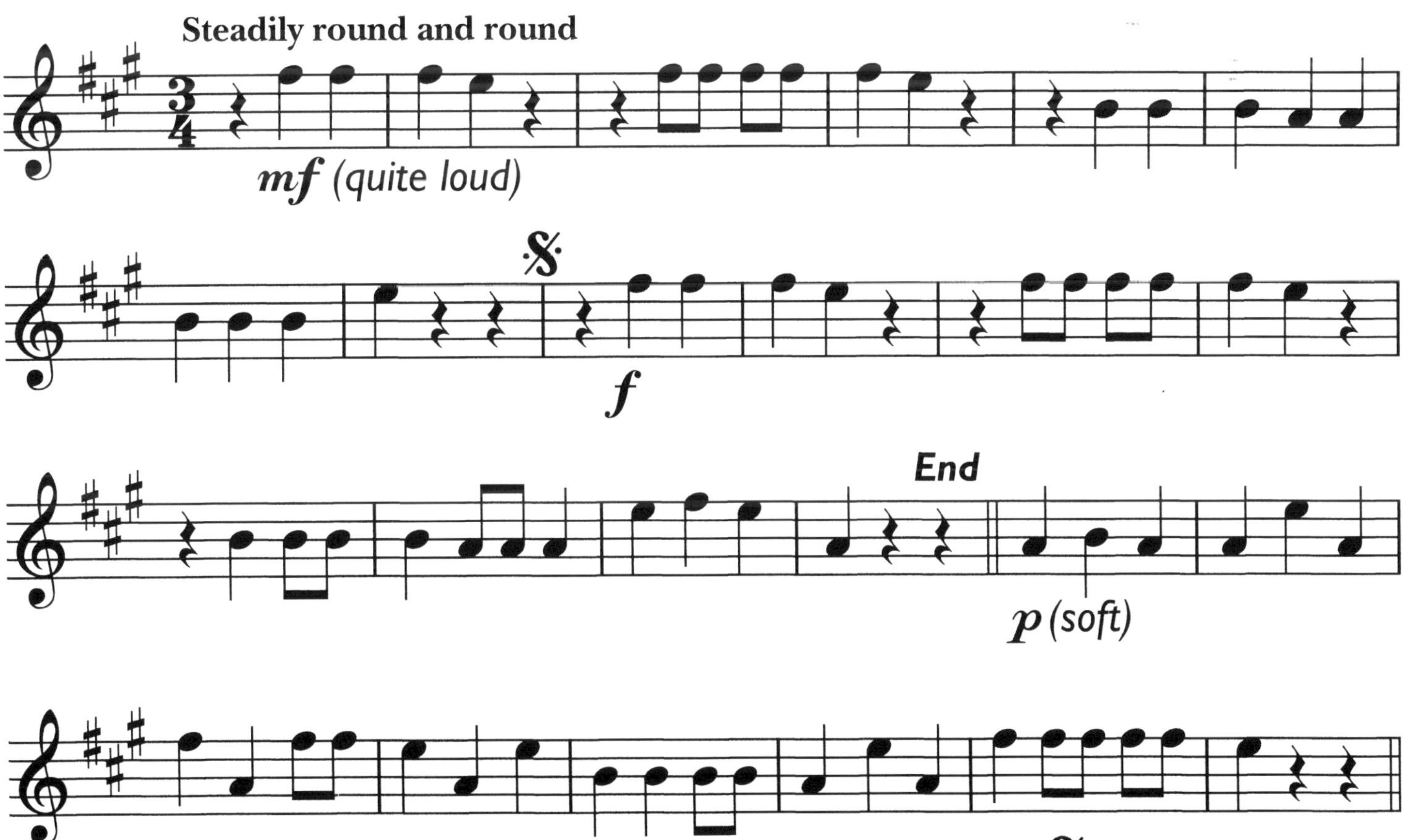

Go back to 𝄋 *and then play to End*

Musical questions and answers with fingers

Listen to the question your teacher or friend plays on the violin. Now make up an answer. Use your fingers, if you can.

Sometimes you should make up the questions for them to answer.

A new note on the E string

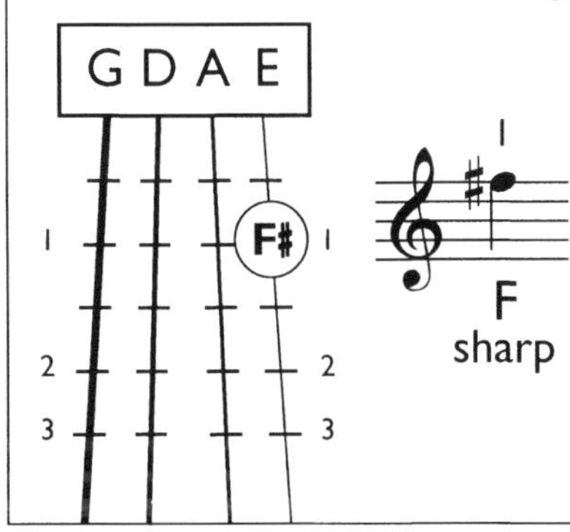

Hot Cross Buns (American style) (**m**i **r**ay **d**oh)

Learn to sing this with your teacher. This is the first of many **m**i, **r**ay, **d**oh tunes you will learn. The simplest way to play **m**i, **r**ay, **d**oh, is to use two fingers for **m**i, one finger for **r**ay, and the open string for **d**oh.

Hot Cross Buns (American style) and *Chocolate Treats* are good together. Find a friend to play *Chocolate Treats* (page 4) while you play *Hot Cross Buns*. You should both use the same string for **d**oh.

Happy or sad?

m **r** **d**
Hot cross buns,
m **r** **d**
Hot cross buns,
d **d** **d** **d** **r** **r** **r** **r**
One a pen-ny, two a pen-ny,
m **r** **d**
Hot cross buns,

mi and **d**oh are copycats (like **s**oh and **m**i). Both sit in spaces, or both sit on lines.

Squirrel (**m**i **r**ay **d**oh)

Learn to sing *Squirrel* with your teacher.

m **m** **r** **r** **d** **r**
Squir - rel in the gar - den
m **m** **d** **d** **r**
Hur - ries past my door,
m **m** **r** **r** **d** **r**
Search-ing for some a - corns
d **d** **r** **r** **d**
For his win - ter store.

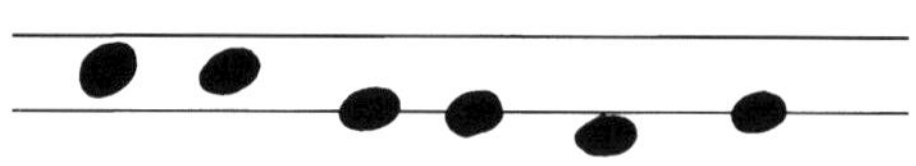

1 See if you can write *Squirrel* on the stave above. The first line has been done for you.

2 Now try making it on your own stave, only this time make **m**i and **d**oh line notes, with **r**ay in the space in between.

Play *Squirrel* on any string you like on your violin, beginning with your second finger.

Jackdaw (mi ray doh)

This piece needs two players. Let your teacher play the lines marked with a penny for now, while you play the lines marked with a jackdaw. Write the solfa letters above the top part in the second line.

A new note on the A string

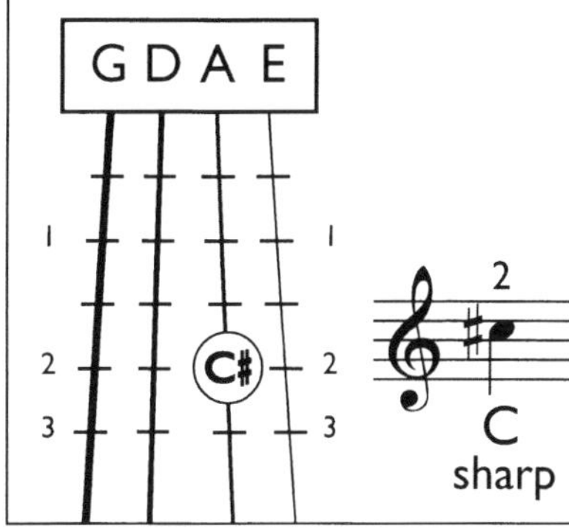

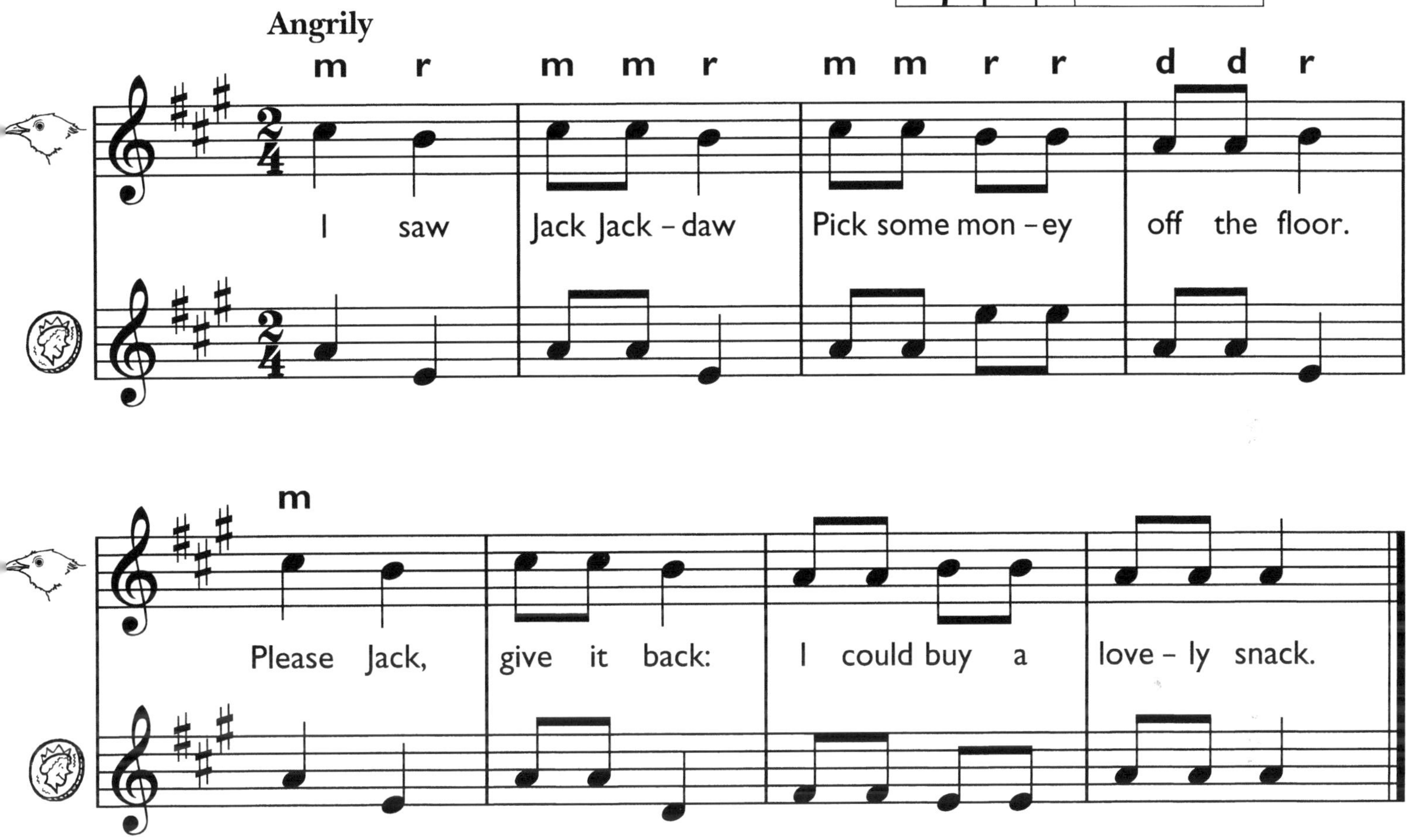

Hoe Down, verse 3

Try playing this first with the bow, then by plucking the strings with the left hand.

Count the introduction:
I 2, **I** 2.

Finding a rhythm

1 Learn *Tall Red Bus* with your teacher, clapping the rhythm as you sing it.

2 Lay out your rhythm cards so that they make the rhythm of *Tall Red Bus*. Tap and say your rhythm to see if it sounds right.

3 Copy the rhythm from your cards into the space provided. (The last line has been done for you.)

Tall Red Bus

d **r** **m**
Tall red bus

r **r** **r** **r** **m**
Com-ing to a stop.

d **d** **r** **r** **d** **d** **d**
Peo-ple on the low-er deck,

m **m** **r** **r** **d**
Peo-ple on the top.

More tunes to play

Find the Open String Tunes on the **activities pages** and try to play *Criss-Cross*.

Find the Get Your Fingers Working pieces on the **activities pages** and see if you can play:

Merrily We Roll Along
The Grand Old Duke of York
Pease Pudding.

Try playing Part B of *Half Past Three* (page 26).

And don't forget to play the *New Waltz Variations* (page 9).

Checklist

✔ When you can
❑ play Carousel
❑ sing and play Hot Cross Buns
❑ sing and play Squirrel
❑ read and play Jackdaw
❑ play Hoe Down, verse 3, with your bow
❑ play Hoe Down, verse 3, plucking with your left hand
❑ play Criss-Cross
❑ play Merrily We Roll Along
❑ play The Grand Old Duke of York
❑ play Pease Pudding
❑ play Half Past Three (part B)

✔ When you have
❑ played some animal sentences with a good ringing sound
❑ tried Musical questions and answers using fingers
❑ written the music for Squirrel
❑ written the solfa in Jackdaw
❑ worked out the rhythm of Tall Red Bus
❑ played New Waltz Variations

STAGE 6 Moving fingers

Cowboy Chorus (fa mi ray doh)

Learn to sing this with your teacher.

You will be able to play this in many places on your violin, but for now:

fa = 3 fingers **mi** = 2 fingers
ray = 1 finger **doh** = 0 fingers

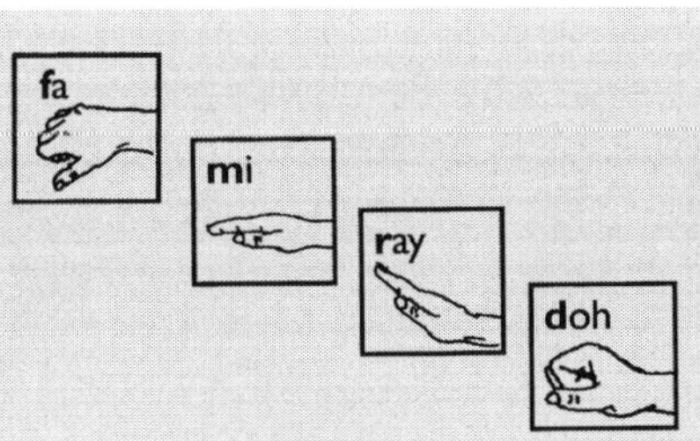

m m m m f f f f

m m m m r r r r

m m m m f f f f

m m m r d - d -

All in a Row (fa mi ray doh)

Sing this piece before you play it.

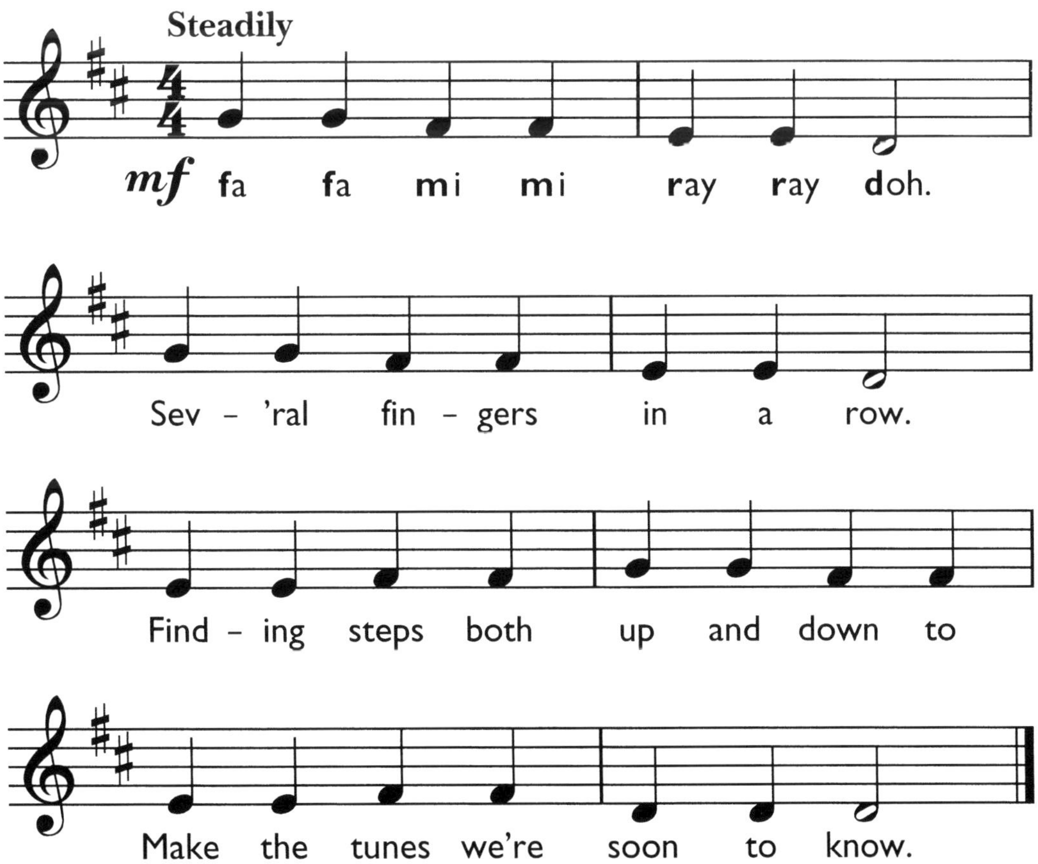

New notes on the D string

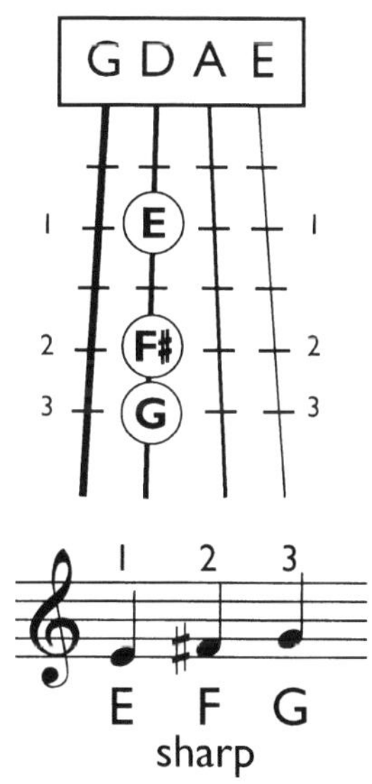

Name this tune

Sing the tune first, then play it on your violin.

Jackdaw and Two-a-Penny

Try playing the bottom part of *Jackdaw* (page 19) and *Two-a-Penny* (page 13), while your teacher (or a friend) plays the top part.

Circles

Sing this tune first, using the solfa names.

> Watch out for the key change. This means that **d**oh shifts from the D string to the A string.

Play each line a little faster than the one before

When you know the second half, try playing your E string between each note without lifting your fingers. Your bow hand will draw little circles. This part of the piece will sound really difficult.

Two into One

Sing these tunes until you know them well.

You can make them into a duet if you sing or play one of them while your teacher sings or plays the other.

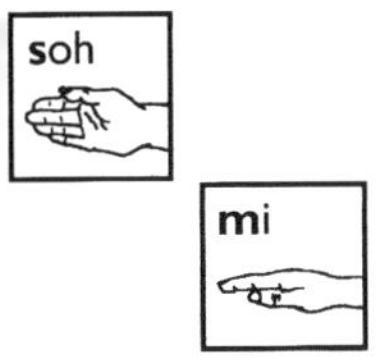

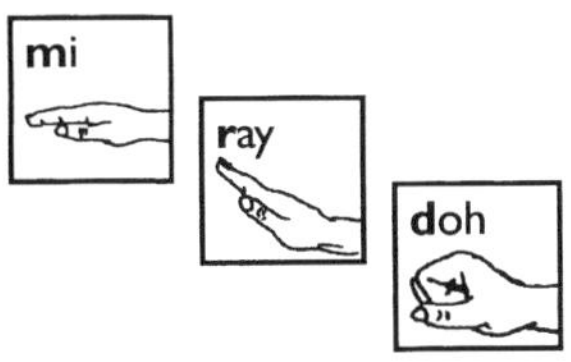

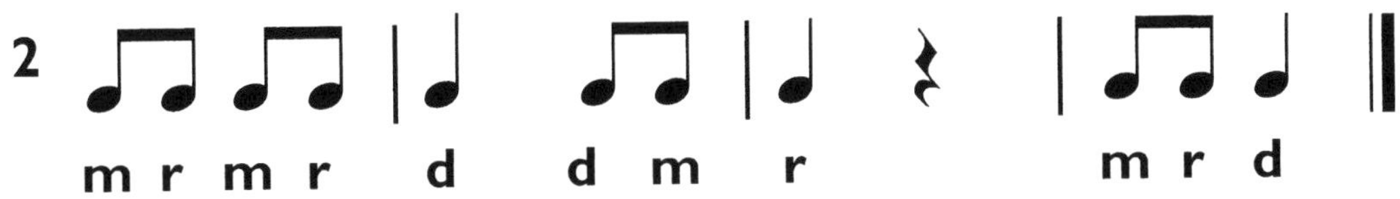

Happy or sad?

Hoe Down, verses 4 and 5

When you have learnt verses 4 and 5 of *Hoe Down* see if you can play every verse followed by the chorus. It will make the longest piece you have ever played.

Not too fast

Now play the CHORUS from memory

Not too fast

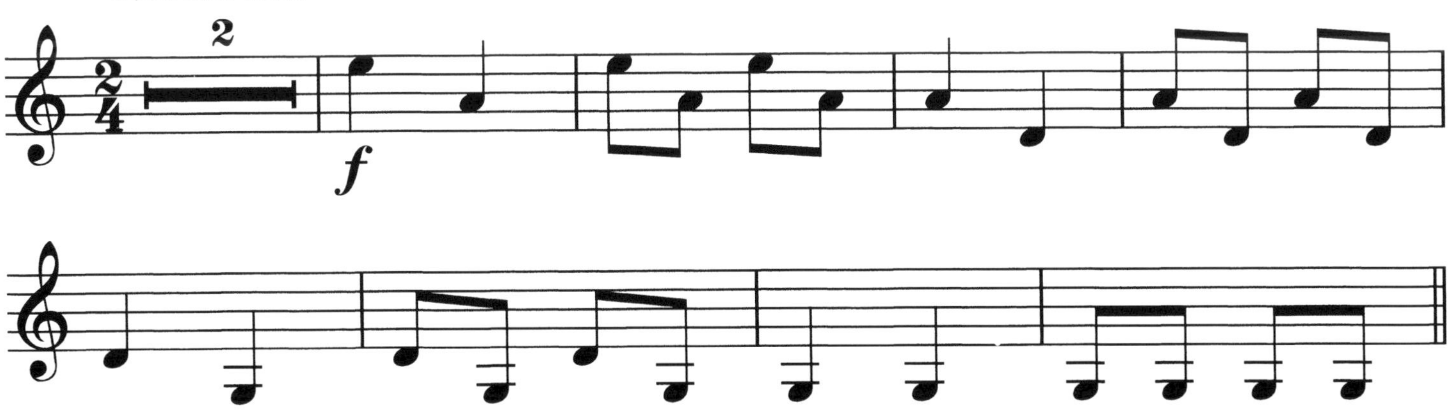

Now play the CHORUS from memory

Nearly Asleep

Ostinato

An **ostinato** is a short pattern repeated over and over again. You must sing or clap this pattern and at the same time listen to how it fits together with a song. Here are two ostinatos for you to try.

Melodic ostinato

Ask someone to sing *Snowman*, while you repeat this ostinato. Now swap round.

Rhythmic ostinato

Now try doing two things at once. Clap this ostinato four times while you sing *Tall Red Bus*.

Compose a song

First, say the rhythm names and then the words in rhythm.

solfa ....

Help! I'm a-bout to sneeze.

solfa ....

Could you pass a tis-sue, please!

Use **m**i, **r**ay and **d**oh in any order to make your tune.

Sing your melody to see if you like it. Change the sounds round to see if it sounds better. When you have a version you like, write the solfa above the rhythm. Then play it.

Hear my rhythm

Can you make a secret 4-beat rhythm with your rhythm cards?

Now clap or play it, and ask someone to say the rhythm back to you.

Did they get it right?

Now swap places.

More tunes to play

Now that you can use your fingers, you will be able to play all these tunes on the **activities pages**:

Twinkle, Twinkle
Lavender's Blue
All Aboard with variations
Criss-Cross
Waltzing Scale and
Marching Scale

Three Brave Mice

Half Past Three (A round in three parts)

Checklist

✔ When you can

- ❑ sing and play Cowboy Chorus by heart
- ❑ sing and play All in a Row
- ❑ play the 'penny' part of Jackdaw and Two-a-Penny
- ❑ sing and play Circles
- ❑ sing and play Two into One
- ❑ play Hoe Down, verses 4 & 5
- ❑ play Nearly Asleep
- ❑ play Twinkle, Twinkle
- ❑ play Lavender's Blue
- ❑ play All Aboard
- ❑ play Criss-Cross
- ❑ play Waltzing Scale
- ❑ play Marching Scale
- ❑ play Three Brave Mice
- ❑ play Half Past Three

✔ When you have

- ❑ worked out the name of the tune on page 22
- ❑ written in the solfa for Circles
- ❑ tried the two ostinatos
- ❑ composed your own tune
- ❑ played Hear my rhythm
- ❑ played Half Past Three as a round

Notation of Solfa Tunes

These songs are meant to be taught by rote. The variety of keys used is to remind teachers that all the songs should be sung at many different pitches, just as many of them will be played at different pitches. One song is in compound time but this should not present difficulty to pupils since they will only work on the pitch element in this book.

1. Hot Cross Buns (**mrd**) Chocolate Treats (**d-s**)

2. Marching

3. Raining (**d-s**)

4. Snowman (**s-m**)

5. A Mugs Game (**s-m**)

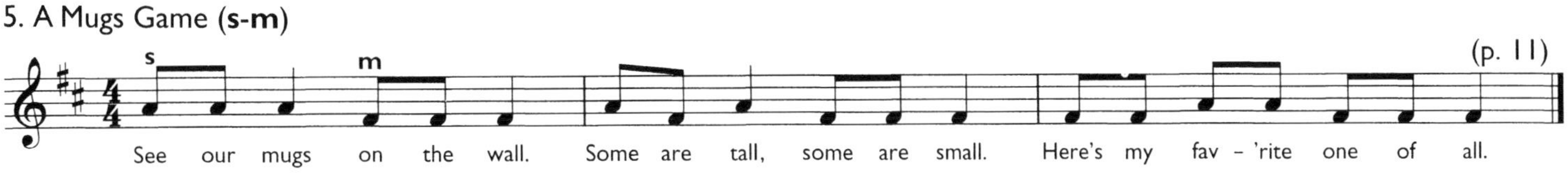

6. Squirrel (**mrd**)

7. Tall Red Bus (**drm**)

8. Cowboy Chorus (**fmrd**)

Happy/sad violinists

The following violinists are sad.

These are the happy violinists:

Rhythm names

Ta		crotchet	quarter note
ti-ti		quavers	eighth notes
Ma		crotchet rest	quarter rest
teke-teke		semiquavers	sixteenth notes
Too		minim	half note

Solfa names

d' = 

(high **d**oh)

t = 

l = 

s = 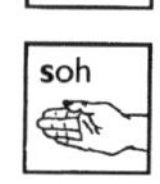

f = 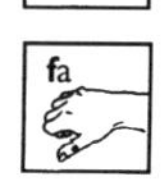

m = 

r = 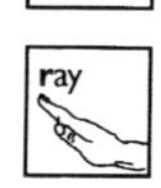

d = 

Reproduced and printed by Halstan & Co. Ltd., Amersham, Bucks., England